ISBN:
979-8-9913997-4-6

"Dedicated to our babies!
May you always know how much you were prayed for
and are prayed over!
May you always create
positive outcomes in this world!"

Special Acknowledgments

Additionally, our team at The Outcome would like to acknowledge all the supporters, volunteers, sponsors and donors that have contributed to this mission since 2020.

We would not have the ability to pour into youth and families without your continued willingness to give of your time, skills and funding!

We pray many blessings upon you and your families as we continue this mission with you!

Special thanks to the Marricle family for their contributions towards
the beautiful illustrations in this title!

We are forever grateful for your support and servant hearts!

I am the outcome
of many things.
But what exactly does that mean?
The outcome is like the end of a story.
I have one, and so do you!
Neither is the same, but both are true.

Jeremiah 29:11 I have good plans for you. Plans to prosper you and not to harm you, plans to give you hope and a future.

I am the outcome
of divine creation.
This means that God created
the heavens, Earth, the sun and stars,
and He even created me.
Think of how special I must be.

Genesis 1:1 In the beginning God created the sky and the Earth.

I am also the outcome
of my family.
All families are different.
Some are small, others are big.
Some are loud and some are quiet.
Some are full of joy in every way, while
others may have some challenging days.

Ephesians 4:32. Be kind and loving to each other. Forgive each other just as God forgave you in Christ.

I am a part of my family,
and it is a part of me.
It doesn't matter what others see,
because my family is unique
just like every animal and tree.

John 15:12. This is my commandment, that you love one another as I have loved you.

I am the outcome
of my community,
meaning the people that
grow up around me.
My friends at school, neighbors down
the street, people I know well,
and some I may never meet.
They all make up the place where I live,
and from them I learn
how to grow and how to give.

Hebrews 10:24. Let us think about each other and help each other to show love and do good deeds.

My community is important,
but my Creator also gave me
my own heart and mind.
I take in what I see, keep all the good
parts and leave any negativity behind.
I am a part of it, and it is a part of me,
but I get to choose
what takes root
and what wasn't meant to be.

Matthew 22:37. Jesus answered, "Love the Lord your God with all your heart, soul and mind."

I am the outcome
of my education,
whether in school, at home
or on my own.
God is my ultimate teacher, and He
gives me many opportunities to learn.
Some things around me are wonderful,
while others may be bad.
I keep the best and learn from the rest.
Whatever is in my future I will earn.

And from my Creator, family,
community and teachers,
I will make my way in life.
When I am ready,
I'll spread my wings and fly,
I will not fear,
I'll be brave and try.

Proverbs 16:3. Depend on the Lord in whatever you do.Then your plans will succeed.

Perhaps one day
I will start my own nest,
in my very own tree,
with those I love best.
And through my own family I will see,
how all along I've been learning,
all that makes me, ME!
I'll teach my children
and they will teach theirs
and through me
a new age of positivity
will be set free.

Psalms 139:14. I praise you because you made me in an amazing and wonderful way.

Because
I am the outcome,
you are the outcome
and together we will
create positive outcomes.
Imagine how special we must be!

John 15:5. I am the vine, and you are the branches. If a person remains in me and I remain in him, then he produces much fruit.

About The Outcome

◆

The Outcome was founded in 2020 by sisters, Nichole Schmalzried and Kayla Sherman out of a God-given vision and burning desire to break generational curses and inspire youth to strive for POSITIVITY, regardless of the challenges the world will always throw at you.

The Outcome serves youth and families in the communities in which Nichole and Kayla call home, but GOD IS SO GOOD and has provided the means and inspiration to carry this message and mission further through this children's book. With each copy purchased Nichole and Kayla pray another child, parent, and family is inspired to grow in their faith and connection with our LIVING GOD!

How will we accomplish our mission?

◆

By focusing on HIS word and guidance;
By providing opportunities and resources that nurture and feed the body, mind & spirit of youth and families;
By encouraging others to join us "on the vine" (John 15: 1-4).

Learn more about The Outcome at
www.iamtheoutcome.net

www.ingramcontent.com/pod-product-compliance
Lightning Source LLC
Chambersburg PA
CBHW041449120626
46547CB00002B/392